WITH JESUS TO THE CROSS

A LENTEN GUIDE ON THE SUNDAY MASS READINGS

—————————— **YEAR B** ——————————

The Evangelical Catholic

SMALL GROUP USER GUIDE

EC THE EVANGELICAL **CATHOLIC**

the WORD among us®
press

Published by The Word Among Us Press
7115 Guilford Drive, Suite 100
Frederick, Maryland 21704
www.wau.org

25 24 23 22 21   1 2 3 4 5

Nihil obstat: The Reverend Michael Morgan, J.D., J.C.L.
                   Censor Librorum
                   November 8, 2017

Imprimatur: + Most Reverend Felipe J. Estévez, S.T.D
                   Bishop of St. Augustine
                   November 8, 2017

ISBN: 978-1-59325-524-4
eISBN: 978-1-59325-526-8

Cover design by Suzanne Earl
Cover image: Compassion I, 1897.
William-Adolphe Bouguereau (1825-1905)
Location: Musee d'Orsay, Paris, France
Photo Credit: © RMN-Grand Palais/Art Resource, NY

Made and printed in the United States of America
Library of Congress Control Number: 2017958190

CONTENTS

Introduction

Behold, now is the acceptable time; behold,
now is the day of salvation.

—2 Corinthians 6:2

How much of life we put off!

"I'll organize that closet someday . . . "

"Tomorrow I'll start a diet . . . "

"I'll quit smoking once I'm past this stressful time . . . "

"I'll repair that _____ when work isn't so busy . . . "

How many people do you know who never quit smoking, never lose weight, never fix things long broken and unattended?

Isn't this true of everyone? We all put off what we know we could and should do.

And don't we do the same thing with God?

"I'll pray regularly once the kids are in school, once they're at college, once they're grown up . . . "

"I'll make a confession another time . . . "

"When I'm not so tired from work, I'll make time to read the Scriptures . . . "

Our hearts may be the thing long broken and unattended, but we don't go to the healer, Jesus, the only one who can help us.

As pressing as the physical parts of life are—health, order, home—how much more important are our supernatural lives! God is love, but how can we experience his love without a relationship with him through Jesus, the one God sent to save us?

God shows us his love within the intimacy that comes through daily time with him, just as it does between people. If we never spend that time, if we have never known the supernatural kindness, generosity, and forgiveness of God, how can we ever hope to be kind, generous, and forgiving toward ourselves or others? How can God help us to grow beyond arrogance, rudeness, self-seeking, or anger? That's what it takes to bear with one another, overcome pride, and become patient—all the things St. Paul described as love in his letter to the new believers in Corinth. Even hope depends on love, and who can live without hope (1 Corinthians 13:1-13)?

If God really so loved the world that he sent Jesus to save us, don't you want that love, no matter the cost? Doesn't love always need to move from our heads to our hearts to be love at all?

It is this movement of your heart that God wants at Lent, not a sacrifice of chocolate or any mere "demonstration" of faith. "'Rend your hearts and not your garments.' / Return to the LORD, your God" (Joel 2:13).

"Behold, *now* is the acceptable time; behold, now is the day of salvation" (2 Corinthians 6:2)—not someday, now.

The Church proclaims these readings every Ash Wednesday to remind us of what we too often neglect. Because we are human beings, the demands of the physical world will always seem more pressing than those of our souls. We need this season to prompt us to put God and our relationship with Jesus at the top of our "to do" lists. We need Lent to inspire us to "rend our hearts."

With Jesus to the Cross can help you stop thinking, "I *ought* to do something for Lent; I *want* to do something," and instead actually do something. Find why the Sunday Readings matter to you *personally*, to the needs and challenges you experience in your own life. God is always trying to say something to you. Reflecting on the Scriptures is the easiest way to hear him. That's why *lectio divina*, prayerful consideration of the Bible, is the time-honored practice for the personal prayer of Christians.

If you're in a small group, praying together and encouraging one another to daily prayer will help you love Jesus more and follow him closely—even to the cross.

Christians believe that the person of Jesus of Nazareth shows us God the Father in a way we can see and understand, because Jesus is God the Son incarnate, living among us as one of us. He is the "light of the world" (John 8:12); without him, we are in darkness about God's love for us and his desire for a relationship with us. Talking to God and prayerfully reading Scripture bring Jesus' light into every part of our lives. It makes us Jesus' disciples, or God's "students," the original meaning of the word "disciple." "If you continue in my word, you are truly my disciples, and you will know the truth, and the truth will make you free" (John 8:31-32). Christ, who is the light of the world, shows you things as they really are, revealing the lies that you are not good enough, smart enough, thin enough, strong enough. Jesus shows you the truth: that we are beloved children of God.

Use this guide to reflect on the words and actions of Jesus and his earliest followers, and you can experience the truth he proclaimed: God's kingdom is indeed "at hand" (Mark 1:15). It's so close to you because it comes through Jesus, who is always waiting for us: "I am with you always, to the close of the age" (Matthew 28:20).

Dive into the Scriptures using this book during Lent, and talk to God through the weekly guides. God can bring forth a great harvest in your life through these practices. Jesus said the word becomes a seed planted in our hearts when we hear it, one that can bring forth a crop thirty, sixty, even one hundredfold (Mark 4:20).

But it's up to you to be the receptive soil where the seed can germinate and take root. Be faithful to a small group or weekly personal reading and to considering the questions. Between meetings or readings, allow God to water and tend the soil of your soul by following the prayer suggestions. Fasting and almsgiving, the other Lenten practices, will fertilize these seeds as nothing else can. When Holy Week comes, let the field of your heart be drenched in the blood of the Lamb and warmed by the resurrection of the Son on Easter. Your life will be transformed.

Now is the acceptable time. Now is the moment of salvation. Don't miss it!

How to Use This Guide

Welcome to *With Jesus to the Cross: Year B*, a guide to help you know Jesus of Nazareth more deeply and understand more fully what his death and resurrection mean in your life.

Weekly Sessions

The weekly sessions use the Sunday Mass readings for Lent to help you enter into the mystery of Christ's life, suffering, and resurrection, the source of our salvation.

Each session includes written opening and closing prayers, the Scripture passages to be discussed that week, ideas for action, and prayer prompts to carry you through the week. Sometimes excerpts from saints, popes, or other great teachers are included that shed light on the message of the gospel.

The sessions in this guide are self-contained. If you or a friend attends for the first time during the third session, there will be no need to "catch up." Anyone can just dive right in with the rest of the group. As with Lent, instead of building sequentially, the sessions deepen thematically, helping you engage more with Jesus and the cross little by little.

The more you take notes, jot down ideas or questions, underline verses in your Bible (if you bring one to your small group, which we recommend!), and refer back to the sessions of previous weeks, the more God has the opportunity to speak to you through the discussion and the ideas he places in your heart. As with any endeavor, the more you put in, the more you get back.

The best way to take advantage of each week's discussion is to carry the theme into your life by following the suggestions in the "Connection to the Cross This Week" section. These prayer prompts will allow Jesus to enlighten your heart and mind on both the challenges of Lent and the joy of the resurrection. If you're discussing the readings with a small group, the facilitator will give you the chance to share experiences from the previous week and talk about the recommendations for the upcoming week during each session.

Each weekly session includes Scripture passages for meditation on the theme of the Sunday readings for that week, as well as the daily Mass readings for the coming week. You can find these in your Bible or online (biblegateway.com, usccb .org, the YouVersion Bible App, and others), or you can use any of the popular free apps that feature the daily Mass readings, such as Laudate or iBreviary. The entire New American Bible is available at the US Conference of Catholic Bishops' website, usccb.org, as well as the daily readings, including an audio version (http://usccb.org/bible/readings-audio.cfm).

Appendices

Helpful appendices supplement the weekly materials. Prior to your first group meeting, please read appendix A, "Small Group Discussion Guide." These guidelines will help every person in the group set a respectful tone that creates the space for encountering Christ together. This small group will differ from other discussion groups you may have experienced. Is it a lecture? No. A book club? No. Appendix A will help you understand what this small group is and how you can help seek a Spirit-led discussion. Every member is responsible for the quality of the group dynamics. This appendix will help you fulfill your role of being a supportive and involved group member.

Appendix B is a resource to enhance and deepen your relationship with Jesus through praying with Scripture. It introduces *lectio divina*, the ancient art of listening to God's voice in his word, and also includes additional methods and tips for building habits of prayer and Scripture meditation.

Appendix C provides a modified version of an extended meditation by St. Ignatius of Loyola, the founder of the Jesuit order. The "Connection to the Cross This Week" section for the Fourth Sunday of Lent encourages you to use this appendix during the week to explore your connection to Christ.

In Appendix D, you will find a guide to the Sacrament of Reconciliation, commonly known as Confession. This sacrament bridges the distance we might feel from God that can come from a variety of causes, including unrepented sin. The Church encourages Catholics to receive this sacrament each Lent, but it is tremendously helpful to receive it even more frequently. If you want to grow closer to Jesus and experience great peace, the Sacrament of Reconciliation is the fast track to get there. This appendix will help alleviate any anxiety by leading you through the steps of preparing for and going to Confession. It also gives suggestions for online resources that provide a way to look at your interior life, traditionally called an "examination of conscience."

Enjoy the adventure!

SUNDAY OF LENT

A Time to Change

The Spirit immediately drove him out into the wilderness.

—Mark 1:12

Opening Prayer

This is an adaptation of the ancient Lenten Prayer of St. Ephrem the Syrian.[1]

In the name of the Father, and of the Son, and of the Holy Spirit.

O Lord and Master of our lives,
keep from us the spirit of indifference and discouragement,
lust for power and idle chatter.

Instead, grant to us, your servants, the spirit of wholeness of being,

---

[1] Adapted from "Lenten Prayer of St. Ephrem the Syrian," Greek Orthodox Archdiocese of America, accessed November 7, 2020, https://www.goarch.org/-/lenten-prayer-of-st-ephrem-the-syrian.

humble-mindedness, patience, and love.

O Lord and King, grant us the grace to be aware of our sins
and not to judge our brothers and sisters;
for you are blessed now and forever.

Amen.

Scripture & Tradition

Reading

Genesis 9:8-15

[8] Then God said to Noah and to his sons with him, [9] "Behold, I establish my covenant with you and your descendants after you, [10] and with every living creature that is with you, the birds, the cattle, and every beast of the earth with you, as many as came out of the ark. [11] I establish my covenant with you, that never again shall all flesh be cut off by the waters of a flood, and never again shall there be a flood to destroy the earth." [12] And God said, "This is the sign of the covenant which I make between me and you and every living creature that is with you, for all future generations: [13] I set my bow in the cloud, and it shall be a sign of the covenant between me and the earth. [14] When I bring clouds over the earth and the bow is seen in the clouds, [15] I will remember my covenant which is between me and you and every living creature of all flesh; and the waters shall never again become a flood to destroy all flesh."

Reading

Mark 1:12-15

[12] The Spirit immediately drove him out into the wilderness. [13] And he was in the wilderness forty days, tempted by Satan; and he was with the wild beasts; and the angels ministered to him.

[14] Now after John was arrested, Jesus came into Galilee, preaching the gospel of God, [15] and saying, "The time is fulfilled, and the kingdom of God is at hand; repent, and believe in the gospel."

Connection to the Cross This Week

On one day before the First Sunday of Lent, think or pray about this short second reading from 1 Peter. The questions will help you meditate on the passage to find what God has to say to you through it.

Reading

1 Peter 3:18-22

[18] For Christ also died for sins once for all, the righteous for the unrighteous, that he might bring us to God, being put to death in the flesh but made alive in the spirit; [19] in which he went and preached to the spirits in prison, [20] who formerly did not obey, when God's patience waited in the days of Noah, during the building of the ark, in which a few, that is, eight persons, were saved through water. [21] Baptism, which corresponds to this, now saves you, not as

a removal of dirt from the body but as an appeal to God for a clear conscience, through the resurrection of Jesus Christ, [22] who has gone into heaven and is at the right hand of God, with angels, authorities, and powers subject to him.

1. What does verse 18 say that Christ did?

In this passage, St. Peter taught Christians in the still very young Church that the God to whom Jesus wants to bring us, his Father in heaven, is the same God of Noah in the Hebrew Scriptures. St. Peter explains the mysterious power of our baptismal waters to bring newness of life, not just when we received the sacrament, but throughout our entire lives. Though we still fail and struggle, Catholics believe that through the sacramental grace of Baptism, we can seek "a clear conscience," and that this comes to us "through the resurrection of Jesus Christ" (verse 21).

2. Do you feel that when you've experienced a clear conscience, it came to you in some way through "the resurrection of Jesus Christ"?

3. What does St. Peter's teaching mean for you, personally? Pray about this. Ask Jesus to show you what your baptism means.

On other days this week, choose one or two of the suggestions on the next page that appeal to you. Plan when you will pray by putting it on your calendar and committing to showing up! This may sound excessive, but scheduling a specific time to do something helps us to accomplish our goals. Can you think of anything you accomplish without first planning for it and then committing time to do it? Prayer is the same, only it's even *more* important! Talking to Jesus connects us to God, the source of everything real and good! Scheduling will help you do one or two extra things this week to draw closer to Jesus and begin or build your relationship with him. For help meditating on Scripture, see Appendix B, "A Guide to Seeking God in Prayer and Scripture."

- Most strongly recommended: Spend time praying with the daily readings this week. The Church chose them for Lent very intentionally to lead you into deeper conversion. Nothing will draw you into the saving mystery of Jesus' death and resurrection as spending time with him by prayerfully reading the Scriptures and talking to God about them. You will find the Mass readings listed on the opposite page and at the end of every chapter. Search "daily Mass readings" on the Internet to have them with you on a device whenever and wherever you need them. (The USCCB website provides the daily readings in a convenient format, and you can listen to them read aloud as well.)

- Appendix B describes *lectio divina*, a Scripture prayer method from the ancient Church helpful for hearing God speak into our hearts. This practice will enrich and challenge you and bring comfort into your life.

- Write St. Ephrem's prayer, or one or two lines from it, on a note card and tape it to your bathroom mirror or your car dashboard. Let this remind you to pray it every day this week so that the saint's words can inspire you to be faithful to your spiritual goals for Lent.

- Go to a daily Mass this week. Let it be something of a journey into the wilderness of God and away from the busyness of your day.

This Week's Mass Readings

Monday
- Leviticus 19:1-2, 11-18
- Psalm 19:8-10, 15
- Matthew 25:31-46

Tuesday:
- Isaiah 55:10-11
- Psalm 34:4-7, 16-19
- Matthew 6:7-15

Wednesday
- Jonah 3:1-10
- Psalm 51:3-4, 12-13, 18-19
- Luke 11:29-32

Thursday
- Esther C:12, 14-16, 23-25
- Psalm 138:1-3, 7-8
- Matthew 7:7-12

Friday
- Ezekiel 18:21-28
- Psalm 130:1-8
- Matthew 5:20-26

Saturday
- Deuteronomy 26:16-19
- Psalm 119:1-2, 4-5, 7
- Matthew 5:43-48

Closing Prayer

In the Name of the Father, and of the Son, and of the
Holy Spirit.

O Christ Jesus, when all is darkness
and we feel our weakness and helplessness,
give us the sense of your presence,
your love, and your strength.
Help us to have perfect trust
in your protecting love
and strengthening power,
so that nothing may frighten or worry us,
for, living close to you,
we shall see your hand,
your purpose,
your will through all things.[2]

Amen.

---

[2] "St. Ignatius of Loyola's Prayer Against Depression," EWTN, accessed
November 3, 2020, https://www.ewtn.com/catholicism/devotions/
prayer-against-depression-378.

SUNDAY OF LENT

A Time to Listen

A cloud overshadowed them, and a voice came out of the cloud, "This is my beloved Son; listen to him."

—Mark 9:7

Opening Prayer

In the name of the Father, and of the Son, and of the Holy Spirit.

Jesus, you ask us to go with you up the mountain.
At the top we stumble on our words;
we look for something to do.

Teach us, Father, how to be still and listen to your Son.
Make our hearts still now;
open them to hear and receive your word—
the Word of Life.

Amen.

Scripture & Tradition

Reading

Mark 9:2-10

[2] And after six days Jesus took with him Peter and James and John, and led them up a high mountain apart by themselves; and he was transfigured before them, [3] and his garments became glistening, intensely white, as no fuller on earth could bleach them. [4] And there appeared to them Eli'jah with Moses; and they were talking to Jesus. [5] And Peter said to Jesus, "Master, it is well that we are here; let us make three booths, one for you and one for Moses and one for Eli'jah." [6] For he did not know what to say, for they were exceedingly afraid. [7] And a cloud overshadowed them, and a voice came out of the cloud, "This is my beloved Son; listen to him." [8] And suddenly looking around they no longer saw any one with them but Jesus only.

[9] And as they were coming down the mountain, he charged them to tell no one what they had seen, until the Son of man should have risen from the dead. [10] So they kept the matter to themselves, questioning what the rising from the dead meant.

Thomas Keating was a Trappist monk and priest who, like other monks in his order, followed the Rule of St. Benedict and practiced periods of silence. His many books teach about contemplation, a way to deepen our relationship with God through silent prayer.

Reading

Jesus in His Divinity is the source of contemplation. When the presence of the Divine is experienced as overwhelming, we are inwardly compelled to contemplate. Such was the situation of the apostles on Mount Tabor when they witnessed the glory of God shining through the humanity of Jesus. They fell on their faces. . . .

Jesus took with him the three disciples who were best prepared to receive the grace of contemplation; that is, the ones who had made the most headway in changing their hearts. God approached them through their senses by means of the vision on the mountain. At first they were overawed and delighted. Peter wanted to remain there forever. Suddenly a cloud covered them, hiding the vision and leaving their senses empty and quiet, yet attentive and alert. The gesture of falling on their faces accurately expressed their state of mind. It was a posture of adoration, gratitude, and love all rolled into one. The voice from heaven awakened their consciousness to the presence of the Spirit, who had always been speaking within them, but whom until then they had never been able to hear. Their interior emptiness was filled with the luminous presence of the divine. At Jesus' touch they returned to their ordinary perceptions and saw him as he was before but with the transformed consciousness of faith. They no longer saw him as a mere human being. Their receptive and active faculties had been unified by the Spirit; the interior and exterior word of God had become one. For those who have attained this consciousness, daily life is a continual and increasing revelation of God. The words they hear in scripture and in the liturgy confirm what they have learned through the prayer that is contemplation.[3]

Connection to the Cross This Week

The second reading on Sunday is Romans 8:31-34. Before Sunday, pray over this passage and consider the questions below.

Reading

Romans 8:31-34

[31] If God is for us, who is against us? [32] He who did not spare his own Son but gave him up for us all, will he not also give us all things with him? [33] Who shall bring any charge against God's elect? It is God who justifies; [34] who is to condemn? Is it Christ Jesus, who died, yes, who was raised from the dead, who is at the right hand of God, who indeed intercedes for us?

1. Do you feel that God is "for you"? Talk to Jesus about any feelings and thoughts about this.

2. St. Paul asks, "Who is to condemn?" (verse 34) because Jesus died for you, his follower, so that you would be freed from condemnation and receive new life. Do you condemn yourself? Others? Talk to Jesus about this area of your life. Ask for his help to grow beyond condemnation of yourself and others.

---

[3] Thomas Keating, OCSO, *Open Mind, Open Heart* (Rockport, MA: Element, 1992), 16–18.

On other days before the next meeting:

If you already pray daily, add silence to your prayer. Try resting quietly in the Lord one day this week. Just turn your inward gaze toward God, and keep refocusing every time you notice you're distracted. You will get distracted—even longtime practitioners of silent prayer experience distractions, and every great teacher on prayer says it doesn't matter in the slightest! Parents' hearts swell with joy when their toddler looks at them with eyes full of love, even for a moment or two, before the child's attention jumps to something else. Our Father God loves us the same way! God created our minds; he knows how they dart from one thing to another.

Many techniques can help us sit comfortably in silent prayer. A simple one is to picture your heart as an empty bowl, tilted out toward God, being wordlessly filled by God. Or you could focus on your breathing: pause for a second after you take in air, and pause for another second before you let it out. The word for "spirit" in the Bible is "breath." God breathed life into us. Our lives depend on our breath. Focusing on it allows you to focus on the Spirit and the reality of life itself in that moment.

You may find these suggestions helpful; if not, skip them! But no matter what you do, trust that you're in the presence of God. Jesus said, "I am with you always, to the close of the age" (Matthew 28:20). Believe him!

If you don't already pray daily, try to pray for fifteen minutes—only one percent of your day—every day this week. If you find the silence challenging, read the Gospel passage for that day (see the list of daily readings on the next page). Think about it. Talk to God about your thoughts, and then rest for a moment or two with God. (For more guidance, see Appendix B, "A Guide to Seeking God in Prayer and Scripture," which explains *lectio divina*, the ancient Christian method of praying with Scripture.) Thank God for the blessings in your life, and close with an Our Father.

This Week's Mass Readings

Monday
- Daniel 9:4-10
- Psalm 79:8-9, 11, 13
- Luke 6:36-38

Tuesday
- Isaiah 1:10, 16-20
- Psalm 50:8-9, 16-17, 21, 23
- Matthew 23:1-12

Wednesday
- Jeremiah 18:18-20
- Psalm 31:5-6, 14-16
- Matthew 20:17-28

Thursday
- Jeremiah 17:5-10
- Psalm 1:1-4, 6
- Luke 16:19-31

Friday
- Genesis 37:3-4, 12-13, 17-28
- Psalm 105:16-21
- Matthew 21:33-43, 45-46

Saturday
- Micah 7:14-15, 18-20
- Psalm 103:1-4, 9-12
- Luke 15:1-3, 11-32

Closing Prayer

In the name of the Father, and of the Son, and of the
Holy Spirit.

Into the silence.
An invitation to the places we keep hidden.
Buried under noise, activity, preoccupation,
there is the quiet place where God waits.
One foot, now another:
descend the stair.

Now, there, in your heart,
breathe the Spirit
who isn't afraid
of your sin,
of your weakness,
of your shame,
but who waits in the very midst of it
to embrace you,
to comfort you,
to burn away
what keeps you apart.

Amen.

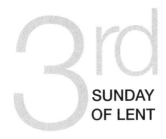

SUNDAY OF LENT

A Time to Believe

"Zeal for thy house will consume me."
—John 2:17

Opening Prayer

Prayer for Guidance by St. Thomas Aquinas

In the name of the Father, and of the Son, and of the
Holy Spirit.

Creator past all telling,
you have appointed from the treasures
of your wisdom
the hierarchies of angels,
disposing them in wondrous order
above the bright heavens,
and have so beautifully set out all parts of the universe.
You we call the true fount of wisdom
and the noble origin of all things.

Be pleased to shed
on the darkness of mind in which I was born,
the twofold beam of your light
and warmth to dispel my ignorance and sin.
You make eloquent the tongues of children.
Then instruct my speech
and touch my lips with graciousness.
Make me keen to understand, quick to learn,
able to remember;
make me delicate to interpret and ready to speak.
Guide my going in and going forward,
and lead home my going forth.
You are true God and true man,
and live for ever and ever.[4]

Amen.

Scripture & Tradition

Reading

Before the Romans destroyed the second temple in AD 70, Jews visited Jerusalem throughout the year, observing religious holidays with animal sacrifices at the Temple. The Temple building and precinct were massive, covering one-sixth of the land area in Jerusalem.[5]

---

[4] "Prayer Before Study," CatholiCity, accessed on March 10, 2017, http://www.catholicity.com/prayer/prayer-before-study.html.

[5] The painting "Reconstruction of Jerusalem and the Temple of Herod" conveys the enormity of the Temple during Jesus' time. You can find an image of it here: https://www.brooklynmuseum.org/opencollection/objects/13389.

The Court of the Gentiles where this Gospel story takes place was part of the Temple complex. It contained a large open outdoor area, very crowded with pilgrims, the animals sacrificed for Passover, and priests and Levites directing activity. Traders sold cattle, sheep, or goats to rich Jews; poorer Jews brought their own animals or bought pigeons. The money changers made it possible for Jews to pay the Temple tax since Jews from other lands brought foreign currency. At Passover, the most important Jewish holiday of the year, large numbers of people would have been in the Temple precincts, including Gentile worshippers who were not allowed into the sanctuary.

Reading

John 2:13-25

13 The Passover of the Jews was at hand, and Jesus went up to Jerusalem. 14 In the temple he found those who were selling oxen and sheep and pigeons, and the money-changers at their business. 15 And making a whip of cords, he drove them all, with the sheep and oxen, out of the temple; and he poured out the coins of the money-changers and overturned their tables. 16 And he told those who sold the pigeons, "Take these things away; you shall not make my Father's house a house of trade." 17 His disciples remembered that it was written, "Zeal for thy house will consume me." 18 The Jews then said to him, "What sign have you to show us for doing this?" 19 Jesus answered them, "Destroy this temple, and in three days I will raise it up." 20 The Jews then said, "It has taken

forty-six years to build this temple, and will you raise it up in three days?" ²¹ But he spoke of the temple of his body. ²² When therefore he was raised from the dead, his disciples remembered that he had said this; and they believed the scripture and the word which Jesus had spoken.

²³ Now when he was in Jerusalem at the Passover feast, many believed in his name when they saw the signs which he did; ²⁴ but Jesus did not trust himself to them, ²⁵ because he knew all men and needed no one to bear witness of man; for he himself knew what was in man.

Reading

1 Corinthians 1:22-25

²² For Jews demand signs and Greeks seek wisdom, ²³ but we preach Christ crucified, a stumbling block to Jews and folly to Gentiles, ²⁴ but to those who are called, both Jews and Greeks, Christ the power of God and the wisdom of God. ²⁵ For the foolishness of God is wiser than men, and the weakness of God is stronger than men.

Connection to the Cross This Week

Commit to praying for fifteen minutes every day this week.

On one day, pray with the first reading for this Sunday that we didn't have time to discuss: Exodus 20:1-17, the Ten Commandments. The commandments can help us to see where and how God is calling us to live our beliefs more fully, or to act more lovingly or with more integrity. Read over them prayerfully, and then ask Jesus about which commandments you could observe better or more wholeheartedly. Ask the Holy Spirit to remind you of specific commandments within your day when you need a reminder. If you struggle with even wanting to change a behavior, ask the Father for the grace to *desire* to observe a commandment more fully and faithfully. On other days, either pray with the daily Mass readings on the next page using the instructions in Appendix B for *lectio divina*, or choose from these suggestions:

- If your belief in the power of the cross feels tepid or uncertain, talk to someone with strong belief this week. Express your own doubts and uncertainty, and ask how that person came to such a firm belief.

- In Catholic tradition, observing Lent includes giving alms. If you haven't given to the poor as part of your Lenten sacrifice, ask Jesus to move your heart with compassion toward the person or organization he wants you to support. If nothing comes to mind, find out how to help in a food pantry or a meal program. Give a gift to Catholic Relief Services, Catholic Charities, or any service organization. If you feel led to give monetarily, go out of your way to give your contribution in secret. Jesus promises that the Father rewards those who give in secret (Matthew 6:1-4).

- If you haven't planned to fast or practice other penances this Lent, think of something you could do this week out of love for Jesus. Perhaps you might skip a meal to spend time with a coworker who seems lonely. Maybe you could visit an elderly family member you rarely see because you don't enjoy being there. Through our penances and acts of service, we concretely choose to love God and others above ourselves.

This Week's Mass Readings

Monday
- 2 Kings 5:1-15a
- Psalm 42:2-3; 43:3-4
- Luke 4:24-30

Tuesday
- Daniel 3:25, 34-43
- Psalm 25:4-9
- Matthew 18:21-35

Wednesday
- Deuteronomy 4:1, 5-9
- Psalm 147:12-13, 15-16, 19-20
- Matthew 5:17-19

Thursday
- Jeremiah 7:23-28
- Psalm 95:1-2, 6-9
- Luke 11:14-23

Friday
- Hosea 14:2-10
- Psalm 81:6-11, 14, 17
- Mark 12:28-34

Saturday
- Hosea 6:1-6
- Psalm 51:3-4, 18-21
- Luke 18:9-14

Closing Prayer

Jesus told us to ask, knock, and seek (Matthew 7:7). Therefore we can do so confidently, even for our own needs and even in front of others in a group. Familiar prayers we all know and can say together have their place, but a new depth comes to group prayer when each of us starts to express our own needs or our gratitude to God directly.

A Time to Choose the Light

The light has come into the world, and people
loved darkness rather than light.
—John 3:19 (NRSV)

Opening Prayer

We will pray the following psalm at Mass next Sunday. It describes the grief of Jewish Temple musicians in exile after they were deported to Babylon. The Babylonians besieged Jerusalem, razed the Temple, and took the religious and political leaders back home with them, a common practice to prevent conquered peoples from rising up again. Jerusalem remained in ruins with a decimated population struggling to survive; Babylon gained a highly educated, musically gifted, and administratively able group of slaves, including the prophet Daniel, the subject of one Old Testament book.

Psalm 137

In the name of the Father, and of the Son, / and of the Holy Spirit.

Leader

By the waters of Babylon, / there we sat down and wept, / when we remembered Zion. / On the willows there / we hung up our lyres.

All

If I forget you, O Jerusalem, / let my right hand wither!

Leader

For there our captors / required of us songs, / and our tormentors, mirth, saying, / "Sing us one of the songs of Zion!"

All

If I forget you, O Jerusalem, / let my right hand wither!

Leader

How shall we sing the LORD's song / in a foreign land?

All

If I forget you, O Jerusalem, / let my right hand wither!

Leader

If I forget you, O Jerusalem, / let my right hand wither! / Let my tongue cleave to the roof of my mouth, / if I do not remember you, if I do not set Jerusalem / above my highest joy!

All

If I forget you, O Jerusalem, / let my right hand wither!

Amen.

Scripture & Tradition

Reading

2 Chronicles 36:14-16,19-23

[14] All the leading priests and the people likewise were exceedingly unfaithful, following all the abominations of the nations; and they polluted the house of the LORD which he had hallowed in Jerusalem.

[15] The LORD, the God of their fathers, sent persistently to them by his messengers, because he had compassion on his people and on his dwelling place; [16] but they kept mocking the messengers of God, despising his words, and scoffing at his prophets, till the wrath of the LORD rose against his people, till there was no remedy. . . .

[19] And they [the Chaldeans, v. 17, another term for Babylonians] burned the house of God, and broke down

the wall of Jerusalem, and burned all its palaces with fire, and destroyed all its precious vessels. ²⁰ He [the king of the Chaldeans] took into exile in Babylon those who had escaped from the sword, and they became servants to him and to his sons until the establishment of the kingdom of Persia, ²¹ to fulfil the word of the LORD by the mouth of Jeremiah, until the land had enjoyed its sabbaths. All the days that it lay desolate it kept sabbath, to fulfil seventy years.

²² Now in the first year of Cyrus king of Persia, that the word of the LORD by the mouth of Jeremiah might be accomplished, the LORD stirred up the spirit of Cyrus king of Persia so that he made a proclamation throughout all his kingdom and also put it in writing: ²³ "Thus says Cyrus king of Persia, 'The LORD, the God of heaven, has given me all the kingdoms of the earth, and he has charged me to build him a house at Jerusalem, which is in Judah. Whoever is among you of all his people, may the LORD his God be with him. Let him go up.'"

Reading

John 3:14-21

¹⁴ "And as Moses lifted up the serpent in the wilderness, so must the Son of man be lifted up, ¹⁵ that whoever believes in him may have eternal life."

¹⁶ For God so loved the world that he gave his only Son, that whoever believes in him should not perish but have eternal life. ¹⁷ For God sent the Son into the world, not to condemn the world, but that the world

might be saved through him. [18] He who believes in him is not condemned; he who does not believe is condemned already, because he has not believed in the name of the only Son of God. [19] And this is the judgment, that the light has come into the world, and men loved darkness rather than light, because their deeds were evil. [20] For every one who does evil hates the light, and does not come to the light, lest his deeds should be exposed. [21] But he who does what is true comes to the light, that it may be clearly seen that his deeds have been wrought in God.

Connection to the Cross This Week

Commit to praying for fifteen minutes every day this week.

Day 1

Use Appendix B to pray for at least fifteen minutes with the Gospel reading for this coming Sunday, John 3:14-21. It's worth revisiting this Scripture passage on our own. We rarely talk openly about the darkness in our lives for obvious reasons: we hide in the darkness what we're ashamed to bring into the light.

During your prayer, talk to Jesus about what you hide. Ask him to help you love him more than the protection of the darkness. Ask for the trust you need to believe that what God has for you in the light will make you far happier than anything else ever could. If God tells you to do anything about this area of struggle, do it immediately, or as soon as possible.

One of the best ways to open our darkness to the light of the world is to share the shadowy areas of our lives with someone else. The Sacrament of Reconciliation provides a safe way to do that. If you're Catholic and you have not already been to Confession this Lent, God longs to help you love the light, his son, Jesus! Nothing has the power to transform pain and shame into abundant life as the presence of Jesus with us in Confession through the priest, acting *in persona Christi*.[6]

If you're squirming right now, you're not alone. It's natural to feel embarrassment or discomfort about Confession. Sin isn't pretty. Something is wrong with us if we don't feel bad when we hurt others, and hurting ourselves packs its own lasting punch, whether we feel guilty or not. Even simply thinking that we haven't done the good God wants us to do leaves us feeling empty and purposeless.

When fear or pride keeps us from Confession, we try to forget our failures and move on. But the effects of sin don't— they remain, hurting us. That's why the Church understands Reconciliation as a healing sacrament. God made us to be in relationships, not alone in our private darkness. He wired us that way. Sin short-circuits the wiring. The grace of Reconciliation powerfully repairs our connection to God and the people in our lives.

You might think, "I don't need to talk to a priest. I talk to God about my sins." Pope Francis says that's like confessing through e-mail!

> Some say: "Ah, I confess to God." But . . . it's like confessing by e-mail, no? God is far away, I say things, and there's no face-to-face, no eye-to-eye contact. Paul confesses his weakness to the brethren face-to-face.[7]

---

[6] This is Latin for "in the person of Christ."

[7] "Pope Francis: Confess Sins with Concreteness and Sincerity," Vatican Radio, October 25, 2013.

Jesus knew how important face-to-face encounter is. Freedom from the darkness doesn't come to us in isolation or exile. Human contact brings us back into human community. It's our way home as surely as the road from Babylon led the deported Jews back to Jerusalem. Jesus made this road when he gave the apostles the power to free people: "Whatever you loose on earth shall be loosed in heaven" (Matthew 16:19). Going to Confession brings us back into communion and guarantees access to that power.

Don't let embarrassment keep you from the healing and consolation that God wants to give you. Appendix D provides a guide to the Sacrament of Reconciliation. If that isn't sufficient to relieve your fears, talk to someone you know who participates in the sacrament and ask them about their experience. Even better, ask if they would accompany you to church when you go to Confession.

If you're not Catholic, the priest is available to you as he is for Catholics. It's very comforting to share the weight of our burdens with another, especially with clergy who are trained and experienced in helping people walk with the Lord.

No matter whether you are a believer, non-believer, Catholic, or other Christian, God loves you and wants you to be with him. "A broken and contrite heart, O God, thou wilt not despise" (Psalm 51:17). Often it's when we're most hurting that we open up to the healing the Lord wants to pour into our hearts and to the only relationship that saves us (John 3:17).

Day 2

Pray with the second reading below before Sunday using the questions that follow.

Reading

Ephesians 2:4-10

[4] But God, who is rich in mercy, out of the great love with which he loved us, [5] even when we were dead through our trespasses, made us alive together with Christ (by grace you have been saved), [6] and raised us up with him, and made us sit with him in the heavenly places in Christ Jesus, [7] that in the coming ages he might show the immeasurable riches of his grace in kindness toward us in Christ Jesus. [8] For by grace you have been saved through faith; and this is not your own doing, it is the gift of God— [9] not because of works, lest any man should boast. [10] For we are his workmanship, created in Christ Jesus for good works, which God prepared beforehand, that we should walk in them.

1. How does St. Paul explain why God sent Jesus, his Son (verses 4-7)? How does he explain it differently than St. John did in John 3:16-17?

2. If you've been baptized, would you say that you've experienced the reality that you have been saved by grace in that sacrament? How could you seek to experience this truth if you haven't?

3. Do you feel that God shows the riches of his grace in kindness toward you, and that happens somehow "in Christ Jesus" (verse 7)? If not, ask God right now

to show you his love in your life, how it has been there in the past, and the ways he is pouring out his love in your life right now. If so, remember times when you've felt sure of the "riches of his grace" and thank God for it.

4. What do you feel would be an appropriate response in your life to the kindness and love that God has shown you? Talk to Jesus about it.

Day 3

For a prayer specifically designed to help us choose light over darkness, see Appendix C. It provides a modified version of an extended meditation from the *Spiritual Exercises* by St. Ignatius of Loyola, the founder of the Jesuit order. "The Two Standards" refers to banners, or flags, on a field of battle that troops rallied around during warfare. (Ignatius was a military man before his conversion; he drew on those experiences for metaphors that could help others grow spiritually.) In "The Two Standards," he asks us to imagine opposing forces of good and evil as armies facing off, each gathered under its own standard.

Other Days

Don't let the fact that there are only three days of prayer suggestions here keep you from praying the other days this week! Do your best to pray every day. On some days, use our suggestions to expand the ways you communicate with God. Think of these as different kinds of activities with God. If you bowled with someone once a week, that relationship would grow if you also decided to meet for coffee and conversation on another day. Similarly with prayer: praying with Scripture allows God to speak to us in different ways than other prayer methods. It will help you get to know Jesus better and deepen your relationship with him.

The daily Mass readings provide an excellent resource for prayer that fits with the liturgical season. To make reading these Scripture passages more prayerful and enriching, use Appendix B, especially the brief instructions on *lectio divina*, an ancient way to pray with the Scriptures.

This Week's Mass Readings

Monday
- Isaiah 65:17-21
- Psalm 30:2, 4-6, 11-13
- John 4:43-54

Tuesday
- Ezekiel 47:1-9, 12
- Psalm 46:2-3, 5-6, 8-9
- John 5:1-16

Wednesday
- Isaiah 49:8-15
- Psalm 145:8-9, 13-14, 17-18
- John 5:17-30

Thursday
- Exodus 32:7-14
- Psalm 106:19-23
- John 5:31-47

Friday
- Wisdom 2:1a, 12-22
- Psalm 34:17-21, 23
- John 7:1-2, 10, 25-30

Saturday
- Jeremiah 11:18-20
- Psalm 7:2-3, 9-12
- John 7:40-53

Closing Prayer

In the name of the Father, and of the Son, and of the Holy Spirit.

(Individual petitions)

All

Lord, make me an instrument of your peace:
where there is hatred, let me sow love;
where there is injury, pardon;
where there is doubt, faith;
where there is despair, hope;
where there is darkness, light;
where there is sadness, joy.

O divine Master, grant that I may not so much seek
to be consoled as to console,
to be understood as to understand,
to be loved as to love.
For it is in giving that we receive,
it is in pardoning that we are pardoned,
and it is in dying that we are born to eternal life.[8]

Amen.

---

[8] "Peace Prayer of Saint Francis," Loyola Press, accessed November 3, 2020, http://www.loyolapress.com/our-catholic-faith/prayer/traditional-catholic-prayers/saints-prayers/peace-prayer-of-saint-francis.

SUNDAY OF LENT

A Time to Die

*"Unless a grain of wheat falls into the earth and dies,
it remains alone; but if it dies, it bears much fruit."*
—John 12:24

Opening Prayer

In the name of the Father, and of the Son, and of the
Holy Spirit.

God our Father, we believe that you are here with us.
We gather as your sons and daughters,
drawn by your Son and enlightened by the Holy Spirit.

Jesus, through our time together,
help us to hear your invitation to follow you more
courageously.

Holy Spirit, open our hearts to the Scriptures,
that through our meditation,

we might desire to give ourselves
more fully and generously
as Jesus did to our Father.

We pray this through Christ our Lord.

Amen.

Scripture & Tradition

Reading

Hebrews 5:7-9

[7] In the days of his flesh, Jesus offered up prayers
and supplications, with loud cries and tears, to him
who was able to save him from death, and he was
heard for his godly fear. [8] Although he was a Son, he
learned obedience through what he suffered; [9] and
being made perfect he became the source of eternal
salvation to all who obey him.

Reading

John 12:20-33

[20] Now among those who went up to worship at the
feast were some Greeks. [21] So these came to Philip,
who was from Beth-sa'ida in Galilee, and said to
him, "Sir, we wish to see Jesus." [22] Philip went and
told Andrew; Andrew went with Philip and they told
Jesus. [23] And Jesus answered them, "The hour has
come for the Son of man to be glorified. [24] Truly, truly,
I say to you, unless a grain of wheat falls into the

earth and dies, it remains alone; but if it dies, it bears much fruit. 25 He who loves his life loses it, and he who hates his life in this world will keep it for eternal life. 26 If any one serves me, he must follow me; and where I am, there shall my servant be also; if any one serves me, the Father will honor him.

27 "Now is my soul troubled. And what shall I say? 'Father, save me from this hour'? No, for this purpose I have come to this hour. 28 Father, glorify thy name." Then a voice came from heaven, "I have glorified it, and I will glorify it again." 29 The crowd standing by heard it and said that it had thundered. Others said, "An angel has spoken to him." 30 Jesus answered, "This voice has come for your sake, not for mine. 31 Now is the judgment of this world, now shall the ruler of this world be cast out; 32 and I, when I am lifted up from the earth, will draw all men to myself." 33 He said this to show by what death he was to die.

Connection to the Cross This Week

It's the last week of Lent. Holy Week begins in the sixth week with Palm Sunday. End your Lent on a high note by praying fifteen minutes every day this week.

Praying with the daily Mass readings not only easily fills that fifteen minutes, but the Scripture passages lead thematically to Holy Week, deepening your experience of Jesus' death and resurrection. Revisit Appendix B if you need a reminder about how to do *lectio divina*.

If you haven't yet made a Lenten confession, plan a time to do it this week. A guide to the Sacrament of Reconciliation appears in Appendix D. If the sacrament still seems too difficult, and you haven't yet reached out to someone who participates in this sacrament, commit to doing that this week. Be sure to ask that person why they go to Confession and what it does for them.

Here are some other ideas for prayer if you need them:

- Take some time every day this week to ask yourself: what do I cling to in place of Christ? This could take many different forms—food, a relationship, a false image of yourself that you project to the world, your own abilities, or a habit of worry. The Lord is indeed the light of the world, but he isn't the kind of God who will force his light into your life. He always entices. We respond by entering into or deepening our relationship with him. Relationships take time. Is there something in your life you want to change to make room for God? Pray about that this week.

  Lift up to Jesus anything you are clinging to as a substitute for what can really satisfy you—Jesus and a relationship with him. You can do this with words or visually. Say something such as this in your own words: "Lord, this is something that keeps me from you, from peace, from living the life of peace you meant for me to live. Help me give this to you, Lord. Please take it from me. I know it is not within my power to 'fix' myself. Only your love can change this. I surrender it to you, O Lord."

  Or if words feel awkward or unnatural, visualize giving yourself to Christ. Imagine him on the other side of a door. Stand on your side of the door, clinging to the thing that keeps you from opening it. Think of the ways you rely on this prop. Does it really accomplish what you want it to accomplish? Does it keep you safe, make you happy, prevent disaster, make you lovable? Try to identify all the hopes that you have placed in this behavior, state of mind, or psychological propensity. When you can see that it has actually given you none of the things you really want, then you will be ready to open the door. Give that thing to which you cling to Jesus, who is standing on the other side. He is waiting to give you what you really need; he can break the power it has had in your life.

- Consider these questions in prayer this week, remembering that Jesus said he would draw all men and women to himself when he was lifted up: What holds me back from Christ? Am I stopping myself from being drawn to him? Do I

  - fear he will take something away from me?

  - find it hard to believe he really is trying to draw me to himself?

  - believe lies that "the ruler of this world" tells me to keep me away from Christ (John 12:31)?

  - doubt that being drawn to him would be the greatest thing that could happen in my life?

This Week's Mass Readings

Monday
- Daniel 13:1-9, 15-17, 19-30, 33-62
- Psalm 23:1-6
- John 8:1-11

Tuesday
- Numbers 21:4-9
- Psalm 102:2-3, 16-21
- John 8:21-30

Wednesday
- Daniel 3:14-20, 91-92, 95
- Daniel 3:52-56
- John 8:31-42

Thursday
- Genesis 17:3-9
- Psalm 105:4-9
- John 8:51-59

Friday
- Jeremiah 20:10-13
- Psalm 18:2-7
- John 10:31-42

Saturday
- Ezekiel 37:21-28
- Jeremiah 31:10-13
- John 11:45-56

Closing Prayer

In the name of the Father, and of the Son, and of the
Holy Spirit.

Lord, we want to give ourselves more fully to you.
You know that our faith is too small,
our vision skewed,
our fears great.
Grant us a supernatural outlook
so that we might see the grain of wheat
in our lives
and want what you want.
Please make us more sensitive to
the ways your Holy Spirit draws us to yourself.
We do not want to miss your invitations.
Please help us to be faithful to your promptings.
We pray for the courage to be molded anew
and the trust to believe the promise of your glory.
We pray this through Christ our Lord.

Amen.

Palm
SUNDAY

The Lord's Passion
A Time to Weep

I gave my back to those who struck me.
—Isaiah 50:6 (NRSV)

Opening Prayer

In the name of the Father, and of the Son, and of the
Holy Spirit.

Behold me, my beloved Jesus,
weighed down under the burden of my trials
and sufferings;
I cast myself at your feet,
that you may renew my strength and my courage,
while I rest here in your presence.
Permit me to lay down my cross in your Sacred Heart,
for only your infinite goodness can sustain me;
only your love can help me bear my cross;
only your powerful hand can lighten its weight.

O Divine King, Jesus,
whose heart is so compassionate to the afflicted,
I wish to live in you;
suffer and die in you.
During my life be to me my model and my support;
at the hour of my death,
be my hope and my refuge.[9]
Amen.

Scripture & Tradition

Reading

Mark 14:17–15:47

[14:17] And when it was evening he came with the twelve. [18] And as they were at table eating, Jesus said, "Truly, I say to you, one of you will betray me, one who is eating with me." [19] They began to be sorrowful, and to say to him one after another, "Is it I?" [20] He said to them, "It is one of the twelve, one who is dipping bread in the same dish with me. [21] For the Son of man goes as it is written of him, but woe to that man by whom the Son of man is betrayed! It would have been better for that man if he had not been born."

[22] And as they were eating, he took bread, and blessed, and broke it, and gave it to them, and said, "Take; this is my body." [23] And he took a cup, and when he had given thanks he gave it to them, and they all drank of it. [24] And he said to them, "This is my blood

[9] "Prayer in Time of Suffering," Catholic Online Prayers website, accessed November 3, 2020, http://www.catholic.org/prayers/prayer.php?p=873.

of the covenant, which is poured out for many. ^{25} Truly, I say to you, I shall not drink again of the fruit of the vine until that day when I drink it new in the kingdom of God."

^{26} And when they had sung a hymn, they went out to the Mount of Olives. ^{27} And Jesus said to them, "You will all fall away; for it is written, 'I will strike the shepherd, and the sheep will be scattered.' ^{28} But after I am raised up, I will go before you to Galilee." ^{29} Peter said to him, "Even though they all fall away, I will not." ^{30} And Jesus said to him, "Truly, I say to you, this very night, before the cock crows twice, you will deny me three times." ^{31} But he said vehemently, "If I must die with you, I will not deny you." And they all said the same.

Reading

$^{14:32}$ And they went to a place which was called Gethsem'ane; and he said to his disciples, "Sit here, while I pray." ^{33} And he took with him Peter and James and John, and began to be greatly distressed and troubled. ^{34} And he said to them, "My soul is very sorrowful, even to death; remain here, and watch." ^{35} And going a little farther, he fell on the ground and prayed that, if it were possible, the hour might pass from him. ^{36} And he said, "Abba, Father, all things are possible to thee; remove this cup from me; yet not what I will, but what thou wilt." ^{37} And he came and found them sleeping, and he said to Peter, "Simon, are you asleep? Could you not watch one hour? ^{38} Watch and pray that you may not enter into temptation;

the spirit indeed is willing, but the flesh is weak."
³⁹ And again he went away and prayed, saying the same words. ⁴⁰ And again he came and found them sleeping, for their eyes were very heavy; and they did not know what to answer him. ⁴¹ And he came the third time, and said to them, "Are you still sleeping and taking your rest? It is enough; the hour has come; the Son of man is betrayed into the hands of sinners. ⁴² Rise, let us be going; see, my betrayer is at hand."

Reading

^{14:43} And immediately, while he was still speaking, Judas came, one of the twelve, and with him a crowd with swords and clubs, from the chief priests and the scribes and the elders. ⁴⁴ Now the betrayer had given them a sign, saying, "The one I shall kiss is the man; seize him and lead him away safely." ⁴⁵ And when he came, he went up to him at once, and said, "Master!" And he kissed him. ⁴⁶ And they laid hands on him and seized him. ⁴⁷ But one of those who stood by drew his sword, and struck the slave of the high priest and cut off his ear. ⁴⁸ And Jesus said to them, "Have you come out as against a robber, with swords and clubs to capture me? ⁴⁹ Day after day I was with you in the temple teaching, and you did not seize me. But let the scriptures be fulfilled." ⁵⁰ And they all forsook him, and fled.

⁵¹ And a young man followed him, with nothing but a linen cloth about his body; and they seized him, ⁵² but he left the linen cloth and ran away naked.

Reading

14:60 And the high priest stood up in the midst, and asked Jesus, "Have you no answer to make? What is it that these men testify against you?" 61 But he was silent and made no answer. Again the high priest asked him, "Are you the Christ, the Son of the Blessed?" 62 And Jesus said, "I am; and you will see the Son of man sitting at the right hand of Power, and coming with the clouds of heaven." 63 And the high priest tore his mantle, and said, "Why do we still need witnesses? 64 You have heard his blasphemy. What is your decision?" And they all condemned him as deserving death. 65 And some began to spit on him, and to cover his face, and to strike him, saying to him, "Prophesy!" And the guards received him with blows.

Reading

15:22 And they brought him to the place called Gol'gotha (which means the place of a skull). 23 And they offered him wine mingled with myrrh; but he did not take it. 24 And they crucified him, and divided his garments among them, casting lots for them, to decide what each should take. 25 And it was the third hour, when they crucified him. 26 And the inscription of the charge against him read, "The King of the Jews." 27 And with him they crucified two robbers, one on his right and one on his left. 29 And those who passed by derided him, wagging their heads, and saying, "Aha! You who would destroy the temple and build it in three days, 30 save yourself, and come down from the cross!" 31

So also the chief priests mocked him to one another with the scribes, saying, "He saved others; he cannot save himself. [32] Let the Christ, the King of Israel, come down now from the cross, that we may see and believe." Those who were crucified with him also reviled him.

[33] And when the sixth hour had come, there was darkness over the whole land until the ninth hour. [34] And at the ninth hour Jesus cried with a loud voice, "E'lo-i, E'lo-i, la'ma sabach-tha'ni?" which means, "My God, my God, why hast thou forsaken me?" [35] And some of the bystanders hearing it said, "Behold, he is calling Eli'jah." [36] And one ran and, filling a sponge full of vinegar, put it on a reed and gave it to him to drink, saying, "Wait, let us see whether Eli'jah will come to take him down." [37] And Jesus uttered a loud cry, and breathed his last.

(Silence.)

[38] And the curtain of the temple was torn in two, from top to bottom. [39] And when the centurion, who stood facing him, saw that he thus breathed his last, he said, "Truly this man was the Son of God!"

[40] There were also women looking on from afar, among whom were Mary Mag'dalene, and Mary the mother of James the younger and of Joses, and Salo'me, [41] who, when he was in Galilee, followed him, and ministered to him; and also many other women who came up with him to Jerusalem.

[42] And when evening had come, since it was the day of Preparation, that is, the day before the sabbath, [43] Joseph of Arimathe'a, a respected member of the

council, who was also himself looking for the kingdom of God, took courage and went to Pilate, and asked for the body of Jesus. [44] And Pilate wondered if he were already dead; and summoning the centurion, he asked him whether he was already dead. [45] And when he learned from the centurion that he was dead, he granted the body to Joseph. [46] And he bought a linen shroud, and taking him down, wrapped him in the linen shroud, and laid him in a tomb which had been hewn out of the rock; and he rolled a stone against the door of the tomb. [47] Mary Mag'dalene and Mary the mother of Joses saw where he was laid.

Connection to the Cross This Week

Holy Week provides an opportunity for deeper conversion as we contemplate the passion, death, and resurrection of Christ. We can encounter the Lord in prayer, Scripture, and the sacramental life of the Church. That's why you should meet as a group to discuss the readings for Easter during the Octave of Easter, the eight days following Easter. This will allow you to spend extra time this week praying, reading Scripture, and participating in the liturgies of the Triduum.

Prepare for the Triduum by praying with the particularly rich Holy Week daily Mass readings each day using the *lectio divina* technique described in Appendix B. The full meaning of Easter will be more available to you from meditating on these Scripture passages. Seek what Jesus has to say to you about your failings and sorrows. Talk to Jesus as personally as you can during the "respond" time of *lectio divina*.

In addition to praying with the readings each day, attend the Triduum services. These three Christian high holy days begin on Holy Thursday and culminate on Easter. The beautiful liturgies of the Triduum have the power to bring us into the mystery of Christ's death and resurrection as nothing else.

Plan to begin with the Mass of the Lord's Supper on Holy Thursday night, when the Church marks the institution of the Eucharist by the washing of feet. After Mass, the priest removes the consecrated bread from the church to a chapel of repose where we watch and pray with Jesus as in the Garden of Gethsemane. We leave the tabernacle in church open—an empty space where Jesus should be—to experience our Lord's absence as his followers did after his arrest.

The empty tabernacle, however, symbolizes much more. Jesus emptied himself for us. Before Holy Thursday, meditate on the hymn from Philippians that we read at Passion Sunday Mass:

> Christ . . . did not count equality with God a thing to be grasped, but emptied himself, taking the form of a servant, being born in the likeness of men. And being found in human form he humbled himself and became obedient unto death, even death on a cross. (Philippians 2:5-8)

Consider the emptiness Christ knew standing before the courts, in the praetorium, carrying his cross, nailed to it on Golgotha. Empty yourself to share in his suffering. Clearing out our schedules can be a way to empty ourselves of our busyness, our self-importance, and our habitual activities that can distract us from God. Persevere even if you feel agitated by time that seems "wasted." Not infrequently, busy lives can hide the truth that boredom in prayer is the real reason we don't pray, not our many responsibilities and duties. Self-emptying demands putting aside what usually occupies our internal lives. Be prepared for that to be difficult, and trust that God will do something with this humbling experience!

At the Good Friday prayer service, we commemorate the day Jesus suffered and died by reading or singing the Passion according to John. We venerate the cross, the reminder of what Christ underwent for our salvation, and for Christians, the sign of God's power and wisdom (Week 3). It is the promise that life will triumph over suffering and death. At the end of the service, the priest brings the consecrated bread reserved after Holy Thursday's Mass from the chapel of repose to distribute before blessing and dispersing the congregation.

The Great Vigil on Saturday night officially includes seven readings from the Old Testament[10] and two from the New, as well as baptisms, confirmations, and first Eucharist for the neophytes. It is a long service, but well worth it. Witnessing adult baptism can be an intense and powerful experience even if we don't know the person being baptized. If you can attend this service, do so!

On Good Friday, meditate for at least ten minutes on the following passage by Fr. Henri Nouwen. Consider your own death, as well as Jesus' on the cross.

> We all must die. And we all will die alone. No one can make that final journey with us. We have to let go of what is most our own and trust that we did not live in vain. Somehow, dying is the greatest of all human moments because it is the moment in which we are asked to give everything. The way we die has not only much to do with the way we have lived but also with the way those who come after us will live. Jesus' death reveals to us that we do not have to live pretending that death is not something that comes to all of us. As he hangs stretched out between heaven and earth, he

---

[10] Sometimes pastors choose to proclaim fewer readings. Only three are mandatory.

asks us to look our mortality straight in the face and trust that death does not have the last word. We can then look at the dying in our world and give them hope; we can hold their dying bodies in our arms and trust that mightier arms than ours will receive them and give them the peace and joy they always desired.

In dying, all of humanity is one. And it was into this dying humanity that God entered so as to give us hope.

—Fr. Henri Nouwen[11]

This Week's Mass Readings

Monday of Holy Week
- Isaiah 42:1-7
- Psalm 27:1-3, 13-14
- John 12:1-11

Tuesday of Holy Week
- Isaiah 49:1-6
- Psalm 71:1-6b, 15, 17
- John 13:21-33, 36-38

Wednesday of Holy Week
- Isaiah 50:4-9
- Psalm 69:8-10, 21-22, 31, 33-34
- Matthew 26:14-25

Holy Thursday
- Exodus 12:1-8, 11-14
- Psalm 116:12-13, 15-18

---

[11] Henri Nouwen, *Walk With Jesus: Stations of the Cross* (Maryknoll, NY: Orbis Books, 1990), 70–71.

- 1 Corinthians 11:23-26
- John 13:1-15

Good Friday
- Isaiah 52:13–53:12
- Psalm 31:2, 6, 12-13, 15-17, 25
- Hebrews 4:14-16; 5:7-9
- John 18:1–19:42

Closing Prayer

This week, rather than bringing personal petitions to Jesus, talk to him directly about your experiences during the discussion. You've been meditating together on some of the most compelling texts in the New Testament.

Most of us will have had interior responses from which we could speak to the Lord. Even if your prayer is something as simple as "Jesus, I don't really believe you died for me," giving voice to that opens a space for the Holy Spirit to work within you.

We all fail Jesus and one another at times. Thinking about that today may move you to pray in sorrow for those times. We also feel abandoned by God at times, as Jesus felt on the cross. (His plea, "My God, my God, why hast thou forsaken me?" appears in Matthew 27:46.)

You can be sure that no matter what you feel or think, you're not the only one. We "find" one another when we honestly share what is on our hearts with God and each other. The light breaks through our isolation in darkness (Week 4), revealing that we are not alone but together, the body of Christ, approaching his everlasting light, one step at a time.

Easter
SUNDAY

The Resurrection of the Lord

A Time to Truly Live

You have been raised with Christ.

—Colossians 3:1

Opening Prayer

The Anima Christi of St. Elizabeth Ann Seton

> In the name of the Father, and of the Son, and of the Holy Spirit.
>
> Soul of Jesus, sanctify me.
> Blood of Jesus, wash me.
>
> Passion of Jesus, comfort me.
> Wounds of Jesus, hide me.
> Heart of Jesus, receive me.
> Spirit of Jesus, enliven me.
>
> Goodness of Jesus, pardon me.
> Beauty of Jesus, draw me.

Humility of Jesus, humble me.
Peace of Jesus, pacify me.

Love of Jesus, inflame me.
Kingdom of Jesus, come to me.

Grace of Jesus, replenish me.
Mercy of Jesus, pity me.

Sanctity of Jesus, sanctify me.
Purity of Jesus, purify me.

Cross of Jesus, support me.
Nails of Jesus, hold me.

Mouth of Jesus, bless me in life, in death,
in time and eternity.
Mouth of Jesus, defend me in the hour of death.

Mouth of Jesus, call me to come to thee.
Mouth of Jesus, receive me with thy saints
in glory evermore.[12]

Amen.

Scripture & Tradition

Reading

John 20:1-9

[1] Now on the first day of the week Mary Mag'dalene came to the tomb early, while it was still dark, and saw that the stone had been taken away from the tomb. [2] So she ran, and went to Simon Peter and the

---

[12] Taken from "The Anima Christi of St. Elizabeth Seton," Catholic Tradition, https://www.catholic.org/prayers/prayer.php?p=1141.

other disciple, the one whom Jesus loved, and said to them, "They have taken the Lord out of the tomb, and we do not know where they have laid him." ³ Peter then came out with the other disciple, and they went toward the tomb. ⁴ They both ran, but the other disciple outran Peter and reached the tomb first; ⁵ and stooping to look in, he saw the linen cloths lying there, but he did not go in. ⁶ Then Simon Peter came, following him, and went into the tomb; he saw the linen cloths lying, ⁷ and the napkin, which had been on his head, not lying with the linen cloths but rolled up in a place by itself. ⁸ Then the other disciple, who reached the tomb first, also went in, and he saw and believed; ⁹ for as yet they did not know the scripture, that he must rise from the dead.

Reading

Colossians 3:1-4

¹ If then you have been raised with Christ, seek the things that are above, where Christ is, seated at the right hand of God. ² Set your minds on things that are above, not on things that are on earth. ³ For you have died, and your life is hid with Christ in God. ⁴ When Christ who is our life appears, then you also will appear with him in glory.

Acts 10:34, 37-43

³⁴ And Peter opened his mouth and said: " . . . ³⁷ [T]he word which was proclaimed throughout all Judea, beginning from Galilee after the baptism which John preached: ³⁸ how God anointed Jesus of Nazareth with the Holy Spirit and with power; how he went about doing good and healing all that were oppressed by the devil, for God was with him. ³⁹ And we are witnesses to all that he did both in the country of the Jews and in Jerusalem. They put him to death by hanging him on a tree; ⁴⁰ but God raised him on the third day and made him manifest; ⁴¹ not to all the people but to us who were chosen by God as witnesses, who ate and drank with him after he rose from the dead. ⁴² And he commanded us to preach to the people, and to testify that he is the one ordained by God to be judge of the living and the dead. ⁴³ To him all the prophets bear witness that every one who believes in him receives forgiveness of sins through his name."

Connection to the Cross for Life

Keep the blessings of your Lenten practices in your life by regularly praying with Scripture and receiving the sacraments. Use the daily readings for your *lectio divina*, or work through a book of the New Testament. Commit to that fifteen minutes every day and Jesus will change your life. Who doesn't want that!

The "things that are on earth" that St. Paul mentioned to the Colossians (3:2) include old habits and ways of thinking and living that do not lead to the abundant life Jesus came to give us (John 10:10). Too often we feel that joy eludes us because we don't have the relationship with Jesus that opens us to the Holy Spirit's life-transforming power.

A relationship with Jesus grows in the same way all relationships do: through time and conversation. That's what prayer is: conversation with God. Talking to Jesus honestly, sharing your life, and seeking his response will nurture, build, and expand your relationship with God in ways you could never imagine.

A regular prayer life makes a way for the power of the resurrection to fill our lives. It makes it possible to overcome old habits and mindsets. Prayer is precisely how we can set our minds on what is above—God—rather than the passing things of this life. Habits of sin, the areas of our lives that we haven't surrendered to God, the seeking after what cannot bring happiness—all these are ways we love the darkness rather than the light (Week 4). They keep us from the resurrection life that can make our joy complete (John 15:11).

Seek the power of the resurrection in a new way this year. Pick one part of your life where you feel a pressing need to become a new creation, to let the old fall to the ground, a seed from which something new can be born (Week 5). Commit that part of your life to prayer. Search online to find Scriptures that pertain to that struggle. For example, search "Bible anxiety" or "Bible lust" or "Bible fear" or "Bible depression." Just naming your challenge will give the Holy Spirit an opportunity to work in this area of your life.

This much is certain: you are not the first person who has ever struggled with any challenge you face. Your brothers and sisters in Christ have walked this way before you, and are walking it with you right now. They share Scripture passages online because they want you to have the newness of life they have found.

Pray over one of the Scripture passages you find for a day or two, and then move to the next one. Less is always more when it comes to encountering Christ in the word. Use the guide to *lectio divina* in Appendix B to help you get the most out of prayerful reading. It teaches you how to hear from the Lord through Scripture. *Lectio divina* works!

When you commit to *lectio divina* with the Bible, you open the way in your heart for the Lord to give you "a fresh, spiritual way of thinking" in every area of your life (see Ephesians 4:23). St. Paul assures us that "the weapons of our warfare . . . have divine power to destroy strongholds" (2 Corinthians 10:4). God can bring victory over every challenge you face through your relationship with Jesus, and prayer is how that relationship happens. God will do in you what you can't do on your own.

This beautiful summary of the power of Christ's death and resurrection can help when you need inspiration. Carlo Carretto aimed for a career in politics until the fascists took over the Italian government before World War II. He threw himself into Catholic Action instead, a youth movement that engaged laypeople in advancing the religious and social priorities of the Church. He spent twenty years in a blur of meetings, conferences, and public organizing. Then he left it all to become a contemplative in the desert of North Africa as a Little Brother of Jesus, the community patterned after the way of life of Blessed Charles de Foucauld.

Eventually, Carretto returned to Italy to found a community where laypeople could participate with the brothers in prayer and reflection. He was a popular retreat master and the author of many books, most famously *Letters from the Desert*, which describes his years in an Algerian monastery:

Real death is separation from God, and this is unbearable; real death is faithlessness, hopelessness and lovelessness. . . .

Real death is the chaos where human beings find themselves when they disobey the Father, it is the tangled web to which they are reduced by their passions, it is the total defeat of all their dreams of greatness, it is the disintegration of their whole personality.

Real death is emptiness, darkness, desolation, despair, hatred, destruction. So . . . Christ agreed to enter this death, into this separation, so as to identify himself with all who were in separation, and to save them.

When he touched the depths of their despair, he announced hope with his resurrection.

When he was immersed in their darkness, he made the brightness of the truth burst forth with his resurrection.

When engulfed by the abyss of their lovelessness, he showed them the infinite joy of resurrection love.

By rising from the dead he made all things new. By rising from the dead he opened new heavens. By rising from the dead he opened new life.

—Carlo Carretto[13]

[13] Carlo Carretto, *Carlo Carretto: Selected Writings*, (Maryknoll, NY: Orbis, 1994), 147–48.

Closing Prayer

In the name of the Father, and of the Son, and of the
Holy Spirit.

My Lord God, I have no idea where I am going.
I do not see the road ahead of me.
I cannot know for certain where it will end.
Nor do I really know myself,
and the fact that I think that I am following your will
does not mean that I am actually doing so.
But I believe that the desire to please you does in fact
please you.

And I hope I have that desire in all that I am doing.
I hope that I will never do anything apart from that desire.
And I know that if I do this you will lead me
by the right road,
though I may know nothing about it.
Therefore will I trust you always
though I may seem to be lost and in the shadow of death.
I will not fear, for you are ever with me,
and you will never leave me to face my perils alone.

—Thomas Merton[14]

Amen.

---

[14] Thomas Merton, *Thoughts in Solitude* (New York: Farrar, Straus and
Giroux, 1956), 79.

APPENDICES

Appendix A
Small Group Discussion Guide

A small group seeks to foster an honest exploration of Jesus Christ with one another. For many, this will be a new experience. You may be wondering what will take place. Will I fit in? Will I even want to come back?

Here are some expectations and values to help participants understand how small groups work as well as what makes them work and what doesn't. When a group meets for the first time, the facilitator may want to read the following aloud and discuss it to be sure people understand small group parameters.

Purpose

We gather as searchers. Our express purpose for being here is to explore together what it means to live the gospel of Jesus Christ in and through the Church.

Priority

In order to reap the full fruit of this personal and communal journey, each one of us will make participation in the weekly gatherings a priority.

Participation

We will strive to create an environment in which all are encouraged to share at their comfort level.

We will begin and end all sessions in prayer, exploring different ways to pray together over time. We will discuss a Scripture passage at every meeting. Participants do not need to read the passage beforehand—no one needs to know anything about the Bible in order to participate. The point is to discuss the text and see how it applies to our own lives.

Discussion Guidelines

The purpose of our gathering time is to share in "Spirit-filled" discussion. This type of dialogue occurs when the presence of the Holy Spirit is welcomed and encouraged by the nature and tenor of the discussion. To help this happen, we will observe the following guidelines:

- Participants strive always to be respectful, humble, open, and honest in listening and sharing: they don't interrupt, respond abruptly, condemn what another says, or even judge in their hearts.

- Participants share at the level that is comfortable for them personally.

- Silence is a vital part of the experience. Participants are given time to reflect before discussion begins. Keep in mind that a period of comfortable silence often occurs between individuals speaking.

- Participants are enthusiastically encouraged to share while at the same time exercising care to permit others (especially the quieter members) an opportunity to speak. Each participant should aim to maintain a balance: participating without dominating the conversation.

- Participants keep confidential anything personal that may be shared in the group.

- Perhaps most important, participants should cultivate attentiveness to the Holy Spirit's desire to be present in the time spent together. When the conversation seems to need help, ask for the Holy Spirit's intercession silently in your heart. When someone is speaking of something painful or difficult, pray that the Holy Spirit comforts that person. Pray for the Spirit to aid the group in responding sensitively and lovingly. If someone isn't participating, praying for that person during silence may be more helpful than a direct question. These are but a few examples of the ways in which each person might personally invoke the Holy Spirit.

Time

We meet weekly because that is the best way to become comfortable together, but we can schedule our meetings around any breaks or holidays when many people will be away.

It is important that our group start and end on time. Generally a group meets for about ninety minutes, with an additional thirty minutes or so afterward for refreshments. Agree on these times as a group and work to honor them.

Appendix B
A Guide to Seeking God in Prayer and Scripture

Unless you are convinced that prayer is the best use of your time, you will never find time to pray.
—Fr. Hilary Ottensmeyer, OSB[15]

If only I had the time!

Time—we only have so much of it each day. All kinds of demands chip away the hours. Modern communication and social media increase our sense of urgency. No wonder we experience conflicting desires over how to spend our time.

One thing we all know for certain: relationships require time. Friendships don't form or last unless people spend time together. Marriages struggle when spouses don't make time to talk and listen deeply to one another. Parents who do not prioritize spending time with their children risk painfully regretting that decision down the road. Some things never change. We were made for relationships, and relationships take time.

So how about our relationship with God?

Just as all relationships require time, so too does a deepening friendship with God. What kind of relationship do you have with the person in your neighborhood with whom you've never had a personal conversation? Even if you take out her

---

[15] Br. Francis de Sales Wagner, OSB, ed., *Sacred Rhythms: The Monastic Way Every Day* (St. Meinrad, IN: Abbey Press, 2014), 5.

garbage can weekly because she is disabled, she is an acquaintance, not a friend. Friends spend time together. Jesus called us his friends (John 15:15).

One way we spend time with Jesus is at Mass. This will always be the center, source, and summit of our prayer lives. But without personal time with Jesus outside liturgies, the encounter at Mass can resemble meeting that neighbor at a block party: talking for a few minutes without any deep connection. The mysterious reality of that person remains remote.

How much time should I spend in personal prayer?

A little goes a long way with God. Start small and work up to more. If you're not already in the practice of prioritizing a prayer time daily, start with fifteen minutes if you can. If that proves too difficult, try ten or even five minutes.

Prayer begets prayer. As you experience the fruit of a deeper friendship with the Lord, your desire for God grows. Your heart longs more and more to build your life around prayer rather than just squeezing it in. Hunger for God grows when you taste the sweetness of Jesus' company and experience the joy of a Christ-centered life.

Basics of Spending Time with God in Prayer

Always begin by recognizing that God is with you. He is with you even when you're not paying attention. When you attend to God, you are simply focusing on reality.

St. Teresa of Ávila called prayer "an intimate sharing between friends."[16] Any good friendship involves three things: talking, listening, and simply being together.

---

[16] Teresa of Ávila, *The Book of Her Life,* trans. Kieran Kavanaugh, OCD, and Otilio Rodriguez, OCD (Indianapolis: Hackett Publishing Company, 2008), 44.

1. Talk to God

There is no wrong way to talk to God. Talk about anything on your mind. Keep it real; don't just say what you think a prayerful person should say or what you think God wants to hear. Even saying, "Lord, help me to pray" is itself a prayer.

If you're stuck, keep in mind the first three things we all learn to say as children: "Thank you," "I'm sorry," and "Please." That's a great outline for a chat with God—it's as simple as that!

2. Listen to God

> *Morning after morning / he wakens my ear to hear.*
> —Isaiah 50:4 (NABRE)

No matter how impossible it may seem, you can learn to discern the Lord's voice in your life. It takes practice and guidance, but never forget this promise of Jesus: "My sheep hear my voice, and I know them, and they follow me" (John 10:27). Jesus means what he says—this is attainable!

The fastest way to learn to recognize the voice of God is to read the Scriptures prayerfully. The Bible truly is God's word expressed in human words. With the Holy Spirit coming to our aid, reading it becomes "a life-giving encounter" (*Novo Millennio Ineunte*, 39). On the following pages, a simple outline of *lectio divina* will help you to find out what the Lord wants to say to you through Scripture. *Lectio divina* is a time-tested way of encountering the voice of the living God in Scripture.

3. Be with God

Sometimes words get in the way of deeper communication. St. John of the Cross said, "The Father spoke one Word, which was his Son, and this Word he speaks always in eternal silence, and in silence must it be heard by the soul."[17] The Lord says, "Be still, and know that I am God" (Psalm 46:10).

Begin and end each prayer time with a minute or two of silence to rest in God's presence. You probably won't hear anything audible or even sense anything interiorly, but be confident that God is filling that silence in ways you cannot immediately perceive. Often something can become very clear later in the day after a time of silence in the morning.

Lectio Divina: Putting It All Together

One of the best ways to "talk," "listen," and "be with" God in a single sitting is the time-honored method of praying with Scripture called *lectio divina* (Latin for "divine reading"). This ancient practice has seen dramatic growth in popularity since Vatican II, partly due to the loud and clear call of every pope since the council for laity and clergy alike to discover (or rediscover) this treasure. For example, Pope Benedict XVI said the following:

> I would like in particular to recall and recommend the ancient tradition of *Lectio divina:* the diligent reading of Sacred Scripture accompanied by prayer brings about that intimate dialogue in which the person reading hears God who is speaking, and in praying, responds to him with trusting openness of heart (cf. *Dei Verbum,* 25). If it is effectively promoted, this practice will bring

---

[17] *The Collected Works of St. John of the Cross,* trans. Kieran Kavanaugh, OCD, and Otilio Rodriguez, OCD (Washington, DC: ICS Publications, 1991), 92.

to the Church—I am convinced of it—a new spiritual springtime.

—Pope Benedict XVI[18]

The term *lectio divina* is often associated with St. Benedict of Nursia of the sixth century. The Rule of St. Benedict assigned monks to meditate upon Scripture at specific hours of the day. In the Middle Ages, four steps came to specify the process: *Lectio* (reading), *Meditatio* (meditation/reflection), *Oratio* (prayer), and *Contemplatio* (contemplation or resting in God's presence).

Lectio teaches us to listen intently for a specific word or phrase that stands out, whether boldly or ever so gently. As believers, we trust that the Holy Spirit aids our reading of the Scripture. When something stands out or troubles us in a reading, this is God's personal word for us to think about (meditation) and discuss with Jesus (prayer, or *oratio*).

If you find it difficult to remember the four aspects of *Lectio,* four "Rs" give a simple and memorable description: read, reflect, respond, rest. See more below.

The Four Rs: A Method for *Lectio Divina*

Preparation

Begin with the Sign of the Cross.
Take a moment to be quiet and still.
Ask the Holy Spirit to guide your time.

---

[18] Pope Benedict XVI, Address to Participants in the International Congress Organized to Commemorate the 40th Anniversary of Dei Verbum, September 16, 2005, https://w2.vatican.va/content/benedict-xvi/en/speeches/2005/september/documents/hf_ben-xvi_spe_20050916_40-dei-verbum.html.

1. **Read** the Scripture selection slowly and attentively. Note any word, phrase, or image that catches your attention. It's helpful to read the passage more than once and/or out loud.

2. **Reflect.** Think about the meaning of whatever caught your attention. The Holy Spirit drew you to it for a reason. What line of thought do you pursue in response? Notice any questions that arise or any emotions you experience. Return to the text as often as you wish.

3. **Respond.** Talk to God about the passage, your thoughts, or anything else on your heart. Thank him for the blessings you have received. Ask him for your own needs, as well as the needs of others. Note any changes or actions you want to make. If the Holy Spirit leads you to any resolution or application in your life, writing it down will help you remember. Ask God to help you live it out.

4. **Rest.** Rest a few minutes in silence with the Lord. "Be still, and know that I am God" (Psalm 46:10). This period of rest allows the meditations and prayers of the day to sink down from your mind to your heart, as you linger in the Father's loving embrace.

Tips for Building a Daily Habit of Prayer

Schedule time.

- Aim to spend some time with God in at least one uninterrupted period, not while driving or doing other activities. Don't multitask! Recall how you feel when you're in the middle of a conversation with a friend who suddenly brings out a smart phone and begins texting. It's a good habit to keep God's presence throughout the day when you're doing other things, but also dedicate a specific time to focus solely on God.

- A scheduled time helps build the habit of prayer. Setting a regular time each day is the surest way to make your prayer time happen.

- Pray in the morning if possible.

- Praying and listening to God first thing in the morning is best for many people because nothing interferes with your prayer if nothing else is happening.

- Morning prayer allows you to quite literally "seek first his kingdom" (Matthew 6:33). It also allows you the chance to make up your prayer at some later time in the day if an unforeseen circumstance interrupts your morning prayer time.

- Praying first thing in the morning has been the preferred practice of many saints and Christians throughout history, and Jesus himself often rose before dawn to pray in solitude.

- But pray how and when you can! It's more important to schedule a time each day than to schedule an ideal time you won't keep. If you cannot do your daily prayer time in the morning, we still recommend starting your day with a simple morning offering.

Don't let the "method" get in the way.

The four steps of *lectio divina* can help, but don't let them limit you. Teresa of Ávila called prayer "an intimate sharing between friends." A conversation between friends would be strange and forced if it always followed a routine or formula. Try different ways to talk, listen to, and simply be with God.

Explore other prompts or methods for prayer. For example, use the Our Father or the Order of the Mass as an outline of the various types of prayer and petition.

Sometimes words get in the way of deeper communication. Lovers stare into one another's eyes wordlessly. Parents and children cuddle and say nothing. The only way to hear anyone, including God, is to be silent. Any friendship in which you are never quiet and attentive will eventually dissolve. Begin and end each prayer time with a minute of silence to rest in God's presence.

Additional Tips

- Be yourself and come to God just as you are, not how you think you should be.

- Set achievable goals.

- Don't overlook the human mechanisms that will enable you to be faithful to daily prayer: Put it on your calendar; set the coffeemaker the night before so that it's ready for your morning coffee date with Jesus; make a commitment to ignore social media and email until you've prayed. Put your alarm on the other side of the room so that you don't waste fifteen minutes hitting the snooze bar!

- If you are distracted, simply persevere. Take those distractions to prayer, or write them down so that you can return to them at a better time. Ask your guardian angel to take care of it. God does not mind distractions. It is the love with which we return our focus to him that he desires. Many find it helpful to use a small notebook or journal to help focus their prayer times.

- Use Nextstep, a discipleship resource from The Evangelical Catholic. The step "Meditate on God's Word" teaches *lectio divina* and gives fourteen Scripture verses to use. Go to www.ecnextstep. com/courses/meditateongodsword to get started. Explore Nextstep for more prayer and discipleship resources too!

Do not overidealize your prayer. Most of the time, it won't "feel" perfect or life changing. There will be unexpected interruptions, dryness, distractions, and other things that interfere. You will experience seasons of both joy and struggle in prayer. After a prayer time, resist the temptation to evaluate "how it went." Just be faithful, and over time you will grow in your ability to pray and to follow the subtler promptings of the Spirit throughout your day.

Appendix C
St. Ignatius and the Two Standards

Composed in the sixteenth century by St. Ignatius of Loyola, founder of the Jesuit order, the "Two Standards" is a well-known spiritual exercise that can help you choose light over darkness.[19]

Ignatius spent his early adulthood in the military and was known as a vain, rough-and-tumble adventurer. A cannonball hit him during a battle, seriously injuring his leg and leaving him bedridden for months. When he saw it healing in an unattractive fashion, he ordered it re-broken and set again. This in the age before anesthesia!

Reading for entertainment during many of his months of recuperation, Ignatius noticed something. When he read adventure stories and romances, he was engaged, but the excitement faded fast. He quickly found himself uninterested, dissatisfied, and agitated. On the other hand, if he read about Jesus or the lives of the saints, his interest continued, along with peace and a desire to serve God. This led to a spiritual conversion.

Ignatius left his home and became a begging pilgrim. He also began guiding people through spiritual exercises using Scripture. From this work, he composed his Spiritual Exercises to help people more deeply appreciate the state of the world, what they themselves are really like, and what God wants for them. The "Two Standards" is one of these exercises. Ignatius asks us to imagine the forces of good and evil as armies, each

---

[19] St. Ignatius of Loyola, "The Fourth Day, Meditation on Two Standards" in *Spiritual Exercises of St. Ignatius of Loyola*, trans. Fr. Elder Mullan, SJ (New York: P. J. Kenedy & Sons, 1914), http://www.ccel.org/ccel/ignatius/exercises.xiii.v.html.

gathered under its own flag, or "standard." The army of darkness and the army of light stand opposed on the field of battle. Which side will you stand with?

Ignatius was convinced that the imagination holds a privileged place in the life of prayer. By imagining ourselves in the Scripture stories, or imagining ourselves in situations such as a battle of light and darkness, we give God the opportunity to communicate with us through our feelings and thoughts. At first, imagining a scene may feel more like something you are just making up yourself than something inspired by God. Don't let this discourage you! You will soon start to notice moments when unexpected ideas occur or feelings emerge. That is the Holy Spirit acting in your heart!

Don't let concern over imagining the landscape and characters obscure your interior life. It's your own heart you are really exploring. Ask yourself, "Where is there darkness and where is there light? In what ways do I choose evil over good?"

Ignatius believed people should be given spiritual exercises by a spiritual director. This written version is a compromise, but if you enter it asking God to guide you, the Holy Spirit will be your director. Someday you may want to seek a Jesuit or Ignatian-trained spiritual director to lead you through the entire Exercises. It's a blessed experience that produces great fruit long after the retreat is over.

Before Beginning

Set aside twenty to thirty minutes in a place you won't be interrupted. Read through the whole exercise first to familiarize yourself with the material. This will allow you to move through it with less intellectual concentration. Try to spend most of the prayer time imagining, not concentrating, on the text. The steps are numbered to make this easier. (This is not the same numbering used in the original meditation.)

Collect Yourself and Prepare

Begin your prayer by placing yourself in God's presence.

Take a few deep breaths and remember that God is closer to you than you are to yourself. He suffers none of the illusions to which we are subject, and he looks on us with love, as his children, rather than through the prism of the world.

Ask God for the grace to focus on the feelings the Holy Spirit draws to your attention during this exercise.

Ask the Spirit to reveal to you any tendencies you may have had in the past when choosing between darkness and light. Ask him to show you times when you chose one or the other.

Thank God for any blessings he will give you in this time.

Engage Your Imagination

1. Imagine Jesus Christ and his followers on a glistening green plain where brightly colored tents have been pitched and flags billow in the breeze. Look across the field. Allow yourself to respond emotionally to this sight.

2. Now look into the distance. Imagine Satan with his followers in a deep ravine, all grays and shadows, and the air dead still. Allow yourself to respond emotionally to this sight as well.

3. Ask God to give you the courage to see clearly the face of good and the face of evil.

4. Envision the commanders on both fields of battle.

   - See Jesus as the supreme Commander-in-Chief in the fields of Jerusalem.

   - See the enemy of our human nature, Ignatius' description of Satan, in a Babylonian field— whatever a field of an enemy looks like to you.

5. Ask God to give you knowledge of how Satan deceives you; Jesus calls him the "father of lies" (John 8:44). Pray that you will be guarded against these lies.

6. Ask for knowledge of the true life that the supreme loving Commander shows as well as the grace to imitate him.

7. Imagine the chief of the enemy seated in that great field of Babylon, as in a great chair of fire and smoke, horrible and terrifying.

   - Consider how he summons innumerable demons that he will scatter forth to do his work: some to one city and others to another, and so throughout the world, until they are in every location on earth.

   - Consider how he instructs them, how he tells them to cast out nets and chains.

   - Hear him encouraging his demons to first tempt with a longing for riches, that men and women who gain them may more easily be pumped up with pride by what they own, rather than who they are (vain honor).

- From these three vices, riches, vain honor, and pride, men and women are drawn to all the rest.

8. Now turn to Christ's army. Consider how our Lord puts himself in a lowly place, beautiful and attractive.

   - Consider how the Lord of the entire universe chooses so many persons—apostles, disciples, etc.—and sends them through all the world spreading love and hope to every kind of person: married, single, rich, poor, old, young, laborer, executive.

   - Consider Jesus instructing his servants and friends sent on this expedition, encouraging a desire to help all.

   - See the insults and contempt that the followers of our Lord encounter. From these humility follows.

   - In comparison with Lucifer's armies, there are three means of forming followers: the first, poverty against riches; the second, insults or contempt against worldly honor; the third, humility against pride. From these three come all the other virtues.

9. The following questions may help your meditation. Move on if they don't.

   - Ask Jesus to teach you how his mind works.

   - Ask him to help you see how people who have chosen the light make their decisions.

   - Ask God what these people value and how this guides their choices.

10. After you have imagined all these things, ask Mary, Jesus' mother, and any of your favorite saints to intercede for you.

- Ask Jesus, the Father, and the Holy Spirit to help you learn whatever it is God wants to teach you from this meditation.

Rest with God in your thoughts and feelings. Close by thanking God for any insights you received. Ask God to continue to unfold the graces he wants you to receive from this meditation, and for your heart to be receptive to them.

Appendix D
A Guide to the
Sacrament of Reconciliation

If it has been a long time since you last went to Confession—or if you've never been—you may be hesitant and unsure. Don't let these very common feelings get in your way. Reconciling with God and the Church always brings great joy. Take the plunge—you will be glad you did!

If it will help to alleviate your fears, familiarize yourself with the step-by-step description of the process below. Most priests are happy to help anyone willing to take the risk. If you forget anything, the priest will remind you. So don't worry about committing every step and word to memory. Remember, Jesus isn't giving you a test; he just wants you to experience the grace of his mercy!

Catholics believe that the priest acts *in persona Christi*, "in the person of Christ." The beauty of the sacraments is that they touch us both physically and spiritually. On the physical level in Confession, we hear the words of absolution through the person of the priest. On the spiritual level, we know that it is Christ assuring us that he has truly forgiven us. We are made clean!

You usually have the option of going to Confession anonymously—in a confessional booth or in a room with a screen—or face-to-face with the priest. Whatever you prefer will be fine with the priest.

For more encouragement and guidance, see Nextstep Be Reconciled online at www.ecnextstep.com/courses/bereconciled.

Steps in the Sacrament of Reconciliation

1. Prepare to receive the sacrament by praying and examining your conscience. If you need help, you can find many different lists of questions online that will help you examine your conscience.

2. Once you're with the priest, begin by making the Sign of the Cross while greeting the priest with these words: "Bless me, Father, for I have sinned." Then tell him how long it has been since your last confession. If it's your first confession, tell him so.

3. Confess your sins to the priest. If you are unsure about anything, ask him to help you. Place your trust in God, who is a merciful and loving Father.

4. When you are finished, indicate this by saying, "I am sorry for these and all of my sins." Don't worry later that you forgot something. This closing statement covers everything that didn't come to mind in the moment. Trust God that he has brought to mind what he wants you to address.

5. The priest will assign you a penance, such as a prayer, a Scripture reading, or a work of mercy, service, or sacrifice.

6. Express sorrow for your sins by saying an Act of Contrition. The following is one traditional Act of Contrition you may use. Many other versions can be found online, or you may simply say you're sorry in your own words.

Act of Contrition:

My God, I am sorry for my sins with all my heart. In choosing to do wrong and failing to do good, I have sinned against you whom I should love above all things. I firmly intend, with your help, to do penance, to sin no more, and to avoid whatever leads me to sin. Our Savior, Jesus Christ, suffered and died for us. In his name, my God, have mercy.

7. The priest, acting in the person of Christ, will absolve you of your sins with prayerful words, ending with "I absolve you from your sins in the name of the Father, and of the Son, and of the Holy Spirit." You respond by making the Sign of the Cross and saying, "Amen."

8. The priest will offer some proclamation of praise, such as "Give thanks to the LORD, for he is good" (Psalm 136:1). You can respond, "His mercy endures forever."

9. The priest will dismiss you.

10. Be sure to complete your assigned penance immediately or as soon as possible.

Also from The Evangelical Catholic

Nextstep, Volume 1

We all experience it: a profound gap in our lives and in our world, between what is and what we wish it could be. Try as we might, our efforts to fix this gap on our own inevitably fail. The good news is that we are not on our own. Through Jesus, the Holy Spirit, and the many gifts in the Church, God loves us, heals us, rescues us, and transforms us. *Nextstep, Volume 1* introduces discipleship: the defining "yes" of our lives to Jesus and the daily practices for the ongoing formation of our hearts. Item# BEC6E1

Nextstep, Volume 2

In this continuation of *Nextstep*, we continue the journey of growing in discipleship, looking even more closely at the nature of freedom. Like any good parent, God wants us to grow in human and spiritual maturity as we acquire the tastes of God's kingdom: choosing for ourselves virtue over vice and acclimating to God's ways. *Volume 2* also focuses on showing person-to-person love and care for those individuals the Lord has placed in our lives. Item# BEC6E2

The Way, Part 1

As Catholic disciples of Jesus, we mature to the extent that we allow the heart and habits of Jesus and his people to become ever more our own. This six-session study explores Catholic Christian discipleship: friendship with Jesus, prayer, and devotion to Scripture.

Leader/Individual Guide: Item# BEC5E9
Small Group User Guide: Item# BEC5E8

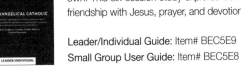

The Way, Part 2

In this second volume of *The Way*, we continue to reflect on our call to know and follow Jesus, particularly through the Eucharist, ongoing conversion, the community of faith, and our call to mission.

Leader/Individual Guide: Item# BEC7E1
Small Group User Guide: Item# BEC7E2

Surrender novena

Believe! Meeting Jesus in the Scriptures
When people "chew" on the word of God through dynamic discussions of the Scriptures, the Holy Spirit reveals the person of Jesus. This guide will encourage everyone, no matter where they are in their spiritual lives, to have a personal encounter with Jesus. The six sessions in this study focus on episodes when Jesus changed people's lives.
Item# BEC1E5

Amazed and Afraid: Discover the Power of Jesus
Amazed and Afraid is designed to help anyone—those who attend church regularly and those who have never met Jesus before in any meaningful way—to dive into the Gospels. Each of the six sessions features a scene about Jesus and his followers, followed by a series of questions, meant to help participants begin to reflect more deeply about their relationship with Jesus. Item# BEC4E7

Signs and Wonders: Encountering Jesus of Nazareth
If we want to know who Jesus is, then we have to discover what his friends said and wrote about him. We can find detailed accounts of Jesus' life—including the signs and wonders he performed—in the Gospels. What better way to explore who Jesus is, or deepen the relationship we already have with him, than to reflect on these accounts? The six sessions include some of the most dramatic Gospel episodes. Item# BEC3E6

With Jesus to the Cross, Year A
This Lent, you are invited to encounter Jesus of Nazareth and to con-template what his life, suffering, and resurrection mean in your own life. Reflecting on the Sunday Mass readings for Lent in the Liturgical Year A, including Palm Sunday and Easter Sunday, you will accompany Jesus as he is led into the desert, transfigured, and betrayed, and in the powerful moment of his resurrection. This guide includes everything you need to lead a small group as a facilitator or to follow the study as an individual. Prepare to fully experience the joy of the resurrection. Item# BEC2E0

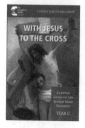

With Jesus to the Cross, Year C
This seven-session guide is designed for those just beginning their faith journey as well as those who want to dive deeper into the Scriptures during Lent. Each session has a "Connection to the Cross" section that encourages participants in a small group to continue their Scripture reading and prayer throughout the week. This guide covers the Sunday Mass readings for Year C from the first Sunday of Lent through Easter. Item# BEC2E6

Walking with God is a series of next steps.

Let Nextstep guide you.

Many people want to grow closer to God, but they don't know how or what to do next. They feel alone, adrift in a world that doesn't even talk about God, with no one to guide them. But God calls everyone into deep, intimate friendship with him. It is possible. Nextstep guides believers step-by-step into the profound, authentic relationship with God they are made for.

You were made for this. Step forward in faith.

Sign up for free and take your Nextstep at **ecnextstep.com.**